Black Bread

Poems, after the Holocaust

BLACK BREAD

POEMS, AFTER THE HOLOCAUST

BY

BLU GREENBERG

KTAV PUBLISHING HOUSE, INC.
HOBOKEN N.J.

Grateful thanks to the following publishers for permission to reprint poems which first appeared in their publications.

The following poems were first published in *Midstream* magazine, which is the publication of the Theodor Herzl Foundation in New York City:

Second Life   April 1976
Wide-eyed Children   April 1976
Cold Feet   February 1978
My Neighbors   March 1978
Love: The Mikvah   February 1979
Black Bread   April 1979
The Holy Ones   June/July 1981

The Yasom was first published in *Sarah s Daughter s Sing*, edited by Henny Wenkart, KTAV, 1990.

Resisting Yom Hashoah, 1985 was first published in *Four Centuries of Jewish Women s Spirituality*, edited by Ellen Umansky and Dianne Ashton, Beacon Press, 1992.

Library of Congress Cataloging-in-Publication Data

Greenberg, Blu, 1936–
   Black bread : poems, after the Holocaust / Blu Greenberg
     p. cm.
   ISBN 0-88125-490-8
   1. Holocaust, Jewish (1939–1945)—Poetry. 2. Holocaust
survivors—Poetry. I. Title.
PS3557.R3782B53 1994
811'.54—dc20   94–18551
                                         CIP

Manufactured in the United States of America
KTAV Publishing House, 900 Jefferson Street, Hoboken NJ, 07030

To
Elie
Renee and Harry*
Lillie and Milton
Sarah and Michael
Gerda and David
Abba* and Vitka
Ebie and Joe
Mietek*
Fanya
Dasha
Henri
Reb Avraham Tzvi* and Helen
Hersh and Fanny*
Betty* and John*
Chris and Miles
Paul*
Gerda
Esther and Leyb*
Goldie and Joe
Sima and Jack
Ben and Vladka
Paula and Joe*
Sigmund and Shoshanna
Emil
Edith
Livia
Frank
Sam and Lilly
Zita and Ludwig*
Gail and Michael
Ursula and Harry
Zalman and Chaya
Hadassah and Yossele*
Ella and Rabbi Samuel*
Chaya Sarah*, Ilana* and Clara

* May their memory be for a blessing

CONTENTS

PREFACE

These poems are mostly about survivors of the Shoah—their stories, their feelings, the way they go about their everyday lives on Earth though once they lived on another planet and arrived on this one with memory intact. It has always seemed to me nothing short of a miracle that a survivor can wake up each morning and get through the day in sanity, even more so with the good cheer and productivity that overwhelmingly characterize survivors' lives. The daily dignity with which they lived their lives in the very midst of such evil, and the decency of their second lives is a testimony to all that is good and noble in the human spirit.

Yet these poems are about a broader group as well, for have we not all been transformed, all Jews who live after the Shoah? Though we do not bear the scars that physical survivors and their descendents do, we carry within us a Holocaust consciousness. At the most ordinary moments of our daily lives, an association with the Shoah or with a fragment a survivor has shared leaps autonomously into mind. In that sense, our internal circuitry has been integrated by the Holocaust factor, now and forevermore.

I have taken a measure of poetic license in this work. While every description is true, the poems include elements of actual events interwoven with products of the imagination and some contain composite elements of more than one life. Thus, resemblance between these poems and the lives of real people is poetic rather than real.

These poems were written over the course of two decades. Here, however, they are compressed into one slender volume that can be read easily in a few hours. I wish that I could ask the reader to proceed at a measured pace and not read more than a few poems at a time; for I fear that one who reads this book in a single sitting may come away with an impression of unbridled morbidity. Yet, incredible as it is, survivors are not given to morbidity. Nor are those others whose orientation to all things has been shaped by the event. Speaking for myself, knowledge of the Shoah has profoundly affected my life but has not overtaken it. It is an ever-present part of me, yet I do not dwell on it. Of course, I am sometimes sad, bewildered, angry, and even morbid—but only sometimes, and, in a relative sense, hardly at all. Far more extraordinary than my personal rhythms is this: Of all of the survivors I know, none of them dwells obsessively on the Holocaust. This is true even of those who have made keeping its memory alive their professional life's work.

The reader may wonder how these poems came to be written. Perhaps an anecdote will explain: In the summer of 1988, on the history-laden campus of Oxford University, I found myself with a few minutes to spare between a conference session that had ended early and a late afternoon appointment to meet my daughter Goody in town. The previous day, Dr. Elizabeth Maxwell of Oxford, conference chairperson, had urged the large body of participants to view a photomontage exhibit, "Terezin," by John Goto, that was being shown in the ground-floor antechapel of Wadham College. A friend whom I met in the halls after the session said he was going, so I joined him.

Having already spent three days listening to the conference proceedings on the Holocaust, I thought I was relatively inured to pain. It was not as if an encounter was unexpected; at some level, I believed I could protect myself. But the exhibit proved otherwise.

Arranged around the room were large-size works, each depicting a different aspect of the agony. Some were oil on canvas; others were enlarged photographs overlaid with blowups from books or official documents. I had almost finished circling the room when I came upon a photomontage containing a paragraph of testimony from a survivor. This eyewitness told the story of two little girls, sisters, ages seven and ten, who had been taken from their parents by the Nazis and were being marched from one place to another. En route, the Nazi guards stopped along a grassy bank. The two sisters, exhausted and hungry, fell asleep on the grass. Suddenly the guard blew a whistle for everyone to get going again. The little sisters awoke and in a dazed panic began to run toward the guards rather than to the point of assembly. For this, the guards shot them as they ran. They fell dead on the green grass while the other children watched, surely in terror and incomprehension, feelings I shared with them forty-five years after the fact.

A few moments later, I went out into the beautiful Oxford sunshine, said good-bye to my friend, and then walked into town. Later that night I described the exhibit to my husband, particularly the scene of the two little girls. He heaved a heavy sigh.

The following day, I sat with my conference group and listened to presentations on the New Testament and the Holocaust. I heard every word against the backdrop of those two little girls.

And that was that. In a few days, the conference was over. Only once since that time, and again today, have I thought about those two little girls. Yet I know that the image is there, permanently embedded under some gray fold. I know that someday, perhaps in two years, perhaps in twenty, a connection will be made, a synapse will relay, and that scene will come straight to the surface. I might be sitting in a park and will notice two little sisters asleep on the grass. Or, I might be reading a newspaper account of a person shot in the stomach while running toward the gunman. Perhaps the scene will suddenly explode into consciousness without any logical connection at all. And will beg to be set down on paper.

There are many people to whom I owe a debt of gratitude: Joel Carmichael, editor-in-chief of Midstream, and Debra Berman and Barbara Zung, formerly of Midstream, for initially publishing several of these poems; Danny Siegel, who shared with our family his love and talent for poetry; Irving Ruderman, for his early interest; Michael Marton, Shlomi Harif, Bob Milch, Bambi Marcus, Carole Sharoff, Natalie Robins, and Moshe Greenberg, for their careful readings and invaluable help: Larry Kamerman, for his wise counsel: poet Henny Wenkart, who polished many of the poems; Diane Schulder Abrams, whose original idea and encouragement it was to collect these poems into one volume; and to J.J. Greenberg, who edited each and every poem with great insight, patience and an extraordinary talent for precision of language.

My deep appreciation goes to Bernard Scharfstein, publisher of KTAV, for his kindness, gracious cooperation and enthusiasm in publishing this book. It has truly been a pleasure to work with him.

I feel a special gratitude to Elie Wiesel. His words and his writings have been an inspiration for my work as they have been for that of so many others. It was he who kept the memory alive until such time as others could also begin to speak.

I wish to thank my husband, Yitz Greenberg. It is not in one manner of meaning alone that I say without him these poems would never have been written, much less published. It was through his interest that I first became open to the

Shoah and through his work and friendships that I came to know many survivors and scholars of the Shoah. Of more immediate nature, he helped me through numerous versions of each poem. And when my confidence in this work flagged, he pressed me forward, a constant story of our lives together.

Finally, I owe the greatest debt of gratitude to the survivors to whom this book is dedicated and whom I have been blessed to count as close friends. From them I have learned so much. They shared their stories, each single tale enabling me to grasp the horror in ways that staggering numbers cannot, each memory bringing me closer to my own Jewish identity, each personal testimony binding me up more intensely with my people.

They have also taught me important lessons about life: that the wellsprings of goodness and humanity, generosity and joy do not dry up, no matter how much evil one has withstood; that it is possible to live with dignity even though all the accoutrements of dignity have been stripped away; that community and family must never be taken for granted; that a heart that has been broken, trashed, and trampled can hold enough love for two complete lives. These are lessons that every human being of every race and religion should carry through life and pass on to future generations.

Riverdale, New York
May 1994

AN ORDINARY BUSINESS MEETING

"Mr. Sheindel here to see you, sir"
Croons Marie, my efficient
Loyal secretary
Her voice pulsing richly
Through the box
Full with promise
Of a new account.

Funny . . .
How she pronounces the name
Shine-*dell*
And mentally
All week long
I've pronounced it *Shane*–dle
Like Shayndle
My sister we all called
Shayneleh
"Little beauty."

We traveled together
In the same cattle car
I, nineteen, strong
Confident this nightmare
Would end tomorrow
Shayneleh, twenty-one
Nursing Menachem Nachum
My first nephew
And last.
Four months of life
Pink-skinned beauty

So good he barely cried
Though there was little milk
And no water
That day, night, day.

But Shayndle had a way with him
A thing to marvel at
When there was nothing
In all the world
To marvel at
That day, night, day.

And then the lights, dogs
Harsh cries, running.
Hastily, a friend whispered
"If she takes the baby
She's finished."

Who could know?
I took the babe
From her reaching
Reluctant arms
Eyes wide
Alternating terror
And hope.

She moved to her line
I to mine.
Moments later
A monster in neat gray
Leashing two dogs with
Eyes more human than his
Snatched Menachem Nachum

From the cradle of my arms
And tossed him
By one leg
Like a chicken
Onto a truck
Of bawling "trash."

Shayndle died one month later
Typhus, grief, and guilt.
One of the lucky ones.

"Ah yes, please
Send Mr. Sheindel
Into my office."

THE MIKVAH

Renewal of the cycle
Expectation and arousal
Women leaving clean and shiny
Young brides and premenopausals.

Alone, at peace, relaxed
Soaking in a warm tub
Before the *tevilah*
Suddenly
I tighten
Remembering that the S.S. would gun
Their motors
Burst into the *mikvah*
Those pure women . . .
Those poor women . . .

My lady of the lake
Checks to see
If I've cut my nails
Removed my lipstick
Flicked off loose hairs
Gone completely under.

"Kosher," she says to me
Kosher again, after the second dip.
A motor slows down outside
My husband coming to take me home.

YIDDISHIST LIBRARIAN WITH A WALRUS MOUSTACHE

A suspenders and belt man
Beneath Monday's brown jacket
Over blue dacron trousers
Or Tuesday's gray jacket
Over brown dacron trousers
And always he wears them
With shiny new knife pleats
Victim of midnight's press
On an old ironing board
With splotched muslin cover.
He wears short-sleeved white shirts
From May to October
No matter the weather
To avoid the frayed cuffs
Of a scholar
On booklover's pittance.

His temples are graying
And pate expanding
Yet brow has not furrowed.
No paunch in the making.
His room's neat as a pin
Washed jars neatly stacked
String wrapped round spooled paper
Not a crumb on the rug
Frayed threads evenly clipped
No detail awry
Not a thing out of place
In the man or his space

Except the walrus moustache
He quietly sports
Year in and year out.

A pleasant fellow
With a rare dash of wit
Wisdom and knowledge
And well-refined speech
But he keeps to himself
(Has an old aunt in Queens
Whom he visits each month
Though she no longer knows him).
He keeps the place quiet
And never makes parties
And pays bills on time.
Suits his landlord *italyaner*
In Woodlands of the Bronx
Never mind the low rent
Or the dark, dark enigma
Is it forty years now?

As he leaves every morning
For the IRT Lex
Fisted coin at the ready
Brown bag for his lunch
Thermos, Yiddish print wrapped
Tucked under his arm
Fresh start on a new day.
He's so kindly polite
With a daily *buon giorno*
To his bathrobed landlady
Out sweeping her walk
And a loud "Merry Christmas"

6

To her ancient squat mother
Who visits biyearly
With big son Alphonso
Who never got married.

Up, up steel-gray steps
Incandescent bulb shadows
Now follow, now lead
As he walks through thin aisles
To loved ones awaiting
Tomes upright or slanted
On tan metal shelves
Worn black leather volumes
Donations from children
Who hide in the suburbs
And clean out dad's shelves
While the body's yet warm.
Now he's searching and sorting
And shelving and noting
These words of a language
Alive yet not living
And not yet reborn.

Noontime, brown-bag time
The shoemaker shod.
Thermos opened by rote
On a two-tiered roll ladder
Arms reach from his stool
Tucked far behind tan shelves
Where bespectacled scholars
Won't disturb him with queries.
Book propped on his knees
He fans out waxed paper

Of Monday's cheese sandwich
Or Tuesday's dark rye
Never lifting his eyes
From the yellowed treasure
Frayed edges glowing
From ancient oil glands
Lest a minute be lost
As he enters anew
A world never left.

It was a love that he learned
At his kind father's knee
From Warsaw's near great
From his uncle, the bachelor
(A Yiddishist librarian)
In a three-story house
First floor, papa's patients.

By themselves on the third floor
In a small room they shared
Twin brother Shmulik
Dapper Dan of Zielna
Though unlike as snowflakes
Together they whispered
Late into the night
Their secrets unfolding
One, all joie de vivre
The other, quite prim
Yet no judgments passed
For brother loved brother.

Twins arriving at camp
This one in fedora

That one in dark suit
The first thing to go
Was Shmulik's moustache
He'd twirled so gaily
Between soft silky finger
This sweet ladies' man
Gone in one day.

Some people give names
To their children's children
Or hang lit bronze plaques
Or dedicate parks.

One incongruously wears
A walrus moustache
That will someday receive
A proper burial
Since hair if not burned
Nor spun into blankets
Can survive for decades
A fitting memorial
To a dear bon vivant.

BLACK BREAD

Black bread
Top seller
At our health food store
Potato peels
Vitamin rich
Says Adelle Davis

Had they known
It kept Jews alive
A few days longer
They would have served
White bread and mashed potatoes

A SPECIAL KIND OF MOTHER

Across the aisle
In a bulkhead seat
Northwest's 131 to Winnipeg
Sits the new kind of mother
Traveling light
With baby and shoulder bag
No bottles
No jars
No fuss
No muss
No bother

She's twenty-five, six, seven
Tawny skinned
Hazel eyed
Dark circles beneath
From baby up all night.

Her light brown
Bangs fall softly
And a pony swings in back
Yet, look, here's a side part
That would surely baffle
101 Ways for Hair Today.

She wears no jewelry or makeup
Except for tiny gold hoops
In small ears
And a hint of shadow
On her lids

Five foot six-seven
Reaching the overhead
With ease and grace
Slender in soft
Prewashed jeans
Good fit
No army-navy surplus here
Her gray sweater vest is
A handmade classic
Topping a pale yellow blouse
All cotton, I am sure
Those fine navy wool socks
Must be her man's
But the neat lizard loafers
Are all hers
Ms. Class

Who Is she?
Earth mother?
Main Line descendant?
Upscale Winnipegger?

Baby
A golden boy
Two fine white teeth old
Frets before takeoff
Softly she talks
Into his tiny ear
He quiets
Then frets again
Across her knee
She straddles him
Rocking her legs
Patting his round bottom

I take in his chubby legs
Dimpled elbows
Blond curls at the nape
And adore him at once.

Now he sits in her lap
Little back
Straight as an arrow
In a cotton T-shirt
Sporting miniature sweat pants
Wide blue stripes up the sides
Matching zipper jacket
Lies on Seat B
A nonsexist pink pacifer
Resting atop.

He cries
A piercing cry
I try to fathom it
Remembering from long ago the
Hungry cry
Tired cry
Earache cry
Fever cry
Temper cry.

As if she's read my mind
She pops the pink pacifier
Into his open mouth
But he'll have none of that
And spits it out.

Now airborne
It's shriek, shriek, shriek.
Just behind me
In Row Seven
Shielded by high-backed seats
Handsome Joe and Jane College
Nuzzle
Facing Jane
Beyond earshot
Of earth mother
Joe says with mock harshness
"Aw, shut up, you little brat"
And Jane giggles adoringly.

Shriek, shriek, shriek
From this small, blond
Blue-eyed tyrant
Mr. First Class
Looks diagonally back
Wanting me to roll my eyes
In camaraderie and shared irritation.

"Do something, woman!"
I say silently
Or I shall forcibly
Gather myself up
And move to Smoking.

Sensing the crowd's mood
She nimbly lifts her vest
Opens a button
And pulls baby toward her
He pulls away

Shrieking again
Perhaps the breast is dry
Or he's got a bellyache
Our sympathy rises.

Back to the breast
She pulls the golden tyke
Peace and quiet descend
Though not perfect stillness
As he sucks noisily
Over the engine's hum.

Why did she wait so long?
No earth mother she
If schedule rules her
Or do those two fine
White teeth hurt?

He drifts off
At the breast
Sleeping undisturbed
As she runs her fingers
Through his golden locks.

We smile again
How I adore
Mothers and babies
Too bad Mr. First Class
Cannot see
Through the bulkhead
This idyllic scene.

Thirty minutes later

Golden boy awakens
Again shrieking
This time, earth mother
Loses not a second
Onto the breast
Ah, blissful peace and quiet.

My mind takes me to the
Hideouts
Where Yocheved and Miriam
Wait with the others
The infant frets and frets
In Yocheved's arms
The lookout lifts
The trapdoor
"They are coming
Shtill, shtill."
Yocheved brings her golden child
To the breast
But there is no milk
Terror sets in
As he cries.

"Ai, we are all goners"
Says her lifelong chum
And best friend
Rolling eyes heavenward.

All eyes are upon Yocheved
And then averted as,
Without luxury
Of a full-throated wail,
She pulls the infant

16

Tighter and tighter
To the breast
Until he cries no more.

A special kind of mother.

CLASS MOTHER

Elena is class mother.
Her nine year old wears dresses
From Bloomie's, Saks.
My nine year old
Wears cousins' hand-me-downs.
My six year old—
The clothes Elena passes on.

Her son is twelve.
Wild, rambunctious, a bull
Whose china shop is the whole world
Yet with the tenderest of hearts.

Elena, blonde and beautiful
So well-mannered and cultured
Generous and good-hearted
Like her husband
Who also wears numbers.

Sometimes
She gossips a bit
Sometimes even
With a bit of sting.
How mild a way
To vent the rage.

briarcliff manor

we're standing inches apart
on the sage-flecked-with-white
carpeting that cushions little falls
and hides muddy scuffs
from oak leaves
the children rustle in
while their parents
sing the *shema*
their eager, open
faces shining
adoring the rabbi
i can see it now.

we're standing in the aisle
under the recessed lighting
between bleached oak pews
a gorgeous cranberry glass
eternal light
shining softly above
while the crowd at adult ed
in their cashmere sweaters
over polo shirts
over trim health club bodies
amble out
to the social hall's collation.

we're standing and chatting amiably
and i'd like to go out for a brownie
but she takes up her tale
unrelated
to the night's lecture
born into a gentile family

neither churchgoers nor antisemites
here we go
i say to myself, warming
(oh, have I come this far?)
to an intermarriage story
with a happy ending.

even as a child
she was drawn to jewish friends
(and there were many in scarsdale)
"intrigued" by judaism
(how? i wonder
as i study the sage carpet
and think of petits fours
disappearing from paper doilies)
dating men jewish and
non jewish alike.

at twenty, at dartmouth
she decides to convert
though not for the love of a man
a true *ger tzedek*
i say to myself
as i look up at her lovely skin
and the tallish man
standing behind her
out of earshot
though surely he's heard this story
a thousand times.

flying home
with the news
her liberal mother

gasps and faints
father hovers nearby
and sweats.

while crossing the atlantic
a pact was made
to take on a danger free
new identity
never to inflict
on their offspring
old vulnerabilities.

WIDE-EYED CHILDREN

We take our children to the memorial.
They begin to ask their own *mah nishtanah*
"How were those years different
From all other years in human history?"
How was Treblinka different from Auschwitz?
Germans from Poles?

I am sorry little children
But you must know it, endure it
For the rest of your lives
I escaped from knowing
Until I was fifteen
Almost sweet sixteen.

Their father has brought them
So they should ask
They already know too much
These tender young shoots
Eyes wide in wonder.

Still it is different
My sweet young children,
For you will never say
"There but for the grace of God" . . .

A VISIT TO OUR FRUITMAN

A glorious spring day
Warm sunniness.
Yesterday's winter-barren Moshulu Avenue
Overnight pregnant with promise.
A maple, starting
To shape its leaf,
Unfurls its tightfisted flag
Clenched from April's snow.
Blue-jeaned steadies of 13–14
Look-alikes
Except for little rises
Here or there.
The babes of last September
Have metamorphosed.
My Moshe, free of mittens, snowsuit,
Scarf, hat, boots.
Moshe's mother
Even freer.
Have I begun to "show"?

Two streets down, two steps up, to our fruitman.

We smile.
"And how are you
  And where were you,
Today, Mrs. Greenberg? Lovely day."
  In thirty-six, thirty-eight
"Fine thank you, Mr. Hoch."
  Forty-one, forty-three?
"And what would you like today?
  Marching proudly with Hitler's youth
Some new white potatoes?

23

Or the einsatzgruppen?
They've just come in."
Where was your father
"Ah, yes. I'll have two pounds."
In thirty-nine?
"And some Idahos?"
With the S.S.?
"Mmm, three pounds.
Or raising his hand
And two pounds of onions."
In grotesque salute?
"I have some nice fresh lettuce here."
A simple citizen just
"It looks good,
Minding his own business?
I'll take a large head." "Good!"
You must have been a perfect Aryan
"Are these melons ripe now?"
With that wheat hair and blue eyes
"This one is ready for tonight."
So tall and strong
"I'll need a larger one.
Did you supervise at the roundup
This young fellow could
With dogs? Or "welcome" the
Eat the whole thing by himself.
Guests at the camp gates?
Right, Moshe?" "He certainly
Surely you've noticed the numbers
Is getting to be a big boy, Mrs. G."
On Mrs. Kaufman's arm
"That he is. And a good boy, too!"
I wonder how she

24

"Anything else for today?"
  Can buy here.
"Just a few tomatoes."
  Is that a Jewish ring your wife wears
"That'll be $7.80."
  Yanked off a slender Jewish finger?
"Here you go."
  Where were you in forty-four
"Thank you, ma'am.
  When Anna was raped in a camp brothel
Here's your change.
  And Lillie's brother, the eye surgeon,
And have a good day
  Gassed till his eyeballs burst
Mrs. Greenberg."
  Do you know what I'm thinking, Mr. Hoch?
"See you again,
  Perhaps tomorrow I'll forget myself, and scream at you.
Mr. Hoch."
  Where were you . . . Where were you . . . Where were you . .
  Where were you . . .

We smile
I walk out
Into the sunlight
Clutching Moshe's small hand
Still wearing
My plastic smile.

THE HOLY ONES

Invite them to your homes
Meetings, parties
Shuls, pools
Inquire after their numbered arms
Nightmares
Sighs, migraines
Do not hush
And never avoid their eyes

Celebrate their accomplished children
Business successes
Decorator wallpaper
Glittering memorial balls
Give them love, pleasure
Time
And listening

For they are the holy ones
Purified in hunger
Sanctified in whippings
Consecrated in the burning last image
Of a bewildered mother
Pulled onto another line
They are our teachers
Our martyrs
Our holy ones
They are our Death
And our Resurrection

COLD FEET

My feet are cold, I cannot sleep
I get up, find a pair of woolen socks.
No one can sleep with cold toes
But they slept every night with frozen toes
Bodies still shivering from icy breaths.

I find an extra-thick pair
My son's soft warm tennis socks
I take an extra blanket
Turn up the thermostat
Knowing, inescapably
Some died from cold feet
Knowing, when they got cold
The Germans warmed them in the fires
Knowing . . .
And even so
I fall cozily asleep.

CATCH

Those people
Up the block
Are perfectly nice
Gina at hill's crest
With five kids
And a husband
Who died by his own hand
The Birds
Whose oft-clipped lawn
As safety valve
For family fights
Testifies to their
True love
Mr. and Mrs. Britton
Who greeted us
On day one
Thirty years ago
With "Say, we once
Met a Jeooo . . ."
All nice people
With New England
Secrets

We live downhill
Last house on the right
Sloping toward the sea
Beautiful whitecaps
Over sparkling
Blue-black waters
Of endless dreams
That draw us here
Year after year

On Shabbos afternoon
Where am I?
Standing in the road
Chatting with Carole who's
Leaning over her high deck.
Uphill, Gina's boys,
Loose laces flying,
Are throwing a wild catch
Missing
The ball races
Toward me
And the steep bank beyond
Then over and down
To splash into the sea
I stand adrift
Eight seconds to act

Catch the ball
Catch the ball
Yell Kim and Jeff
Running
Watching
Waiting
Unaware
There is no *eruv*
In this nice town
Of three hundred years
On the holiest day of my week.

Shall I catch it
But not throw it back?
Can I stop it with my foot
Only half a transgression?

No, all or nothing
Desecrate the Sabbath or the Name
That mean old Jeoooish lady
I stand adrift
Two seconds to act.

Barta's *zayde* died
With his wife
And two unmarried daughters
Al kiddush hashem.
When warning came
To his *shtetl*
To flee in haste
That no-nonsense Jew
Would not hitch
Cart and horse
Till three stars shone
But they came for him
Before *minchah* time.

Shall I catch the ball
To punish God for
That Shabbos afternoon
In Kiev?

Shall I catch the ball
Betraying Barta's *zayde*
And my own?

What would he do
Now?

THREE KOSHER DINERS

By chance
Though nothing's ever
By chance
Next to me
Fitting tightly
Into Seats A and B
Are two of mine

You're "one of us"
Grants Seat B
Though my hair
Is uncovered
As we chat of Montreal
Yeshivas and shuls
And play our favorite—
Jewish geography

"Fasten your seat belts"
And her sheitel
Tilts slightly toward her
Thick eyeglasses
We bond.
What I lived through . . .
My sisters . . .
My husband . . .
(Silent in Seat A)
No one should know . . .

The stewardess brings her
More bad news
We don't have
Your kosher meals

She groans
To her husband
In Yiddish
Never mind, I say
When it comes
I'll share mine
We chat more
Of rabbis and kashrut
And new vacation spots
For *yidden*
Her favorite word

Again the stewardess
This time with
Bad news for me
Found two special meals
For seats A and B
As she passes the trays
Over my spread table
With promises to
Fill out a form

"One of mine"
Breaks the cellophane wrap
And abruptly
Stops our shmoozing
I smell Wilton's chicken
Eye jelly roll sideways

But she lost everything

THE *YASOM*

Yeshiva handsome:
Hooked nose
Gray, gray eyes
Rosy cheeks
Over good bones
Curly brown hair
Under a hat
Tilted slightly back
The perfect chic of a modern yeshiva *bochur*.

He knew how to get around
How to *hondle*
Sniff opportunity
Hail-fellow-well-met.
He was kind, funny, clever
Though at times a bit moody
At times a bit distant.
We knew he had been saved by miracles.

He loved Sarah
The oldest of five daughters
Of a great, booming family.
"No!" said her father
A charitable man,
"A *yasom*
Raised by *rebbes* . . ."
"No," said her mother
A woman of good works,
"Without a father
How will he
Know to be one?"

"Better to wait," said Tante Esther
"Find another," said the wise old *bubbe*.
"No . . ." said my friend
To her Beloved.

The gray eyes darkened
The *yasom*
Straightened his hat.

THERE BUT FOR THE GRACE OF GOD . . .

David.
My beautiful athlete
And fearless adventurer
Born in the sixties
Now a foot taller than I
With one year of growth
Still in him
Shiny face sun-windswept
Languid lean torso
And sturdy long legs
Stretched out on the couch
With Billy Joel blaring
His bittersweet gold

I lower the volume
(Though not all the way
To avoid a teen protest)
And flop into a chair
Tuck my feet under
For a cozy moment
Of 'quality time'.
So how was skiing?
(For a routine opener)

So Steven and I . . .
Down the steepest slope . . .
I'm getting so good . . .
Warm fire in the lodge . . .
Spent all my money . . .
It was so great . . .

Except for this big man
With a thick neck
Standing at the bottom
Pointing us left or right
It felt so eerie
For a second I felt
Real scared.

GENDER RESEARCH

Men, when lost, fall back
on built-in navigational skills
honed from far-off days
of tracking large prey.
Women find their way
by remembering local landmarks
or asking help from strangers.

Men's imagination can twist
three dimensional objects in space
and thus do better in Higher Math.
Women have superior verbal skills
and sharper hearing, taste
smell and touch.

Boys prefer guns
and girls dolls
no matter well meaning efforts
to ply both with unisex toys.

Women prefer to maintain
the edge on nurturing
when one parent
must choose part time work.

Men are more comfortable
wielding power and giving direction.
Women like to lead
by consensus and compromise.

All of these findings
may be challenged in a decade

But one man in Des Moines
already knows the randomness
of such comparisions.

Standing in a long row
between loving parents
he was forced to step forward
the "every other Jew" in Nazi sport
to be sent to the gas.

As the guard moved down the row
Mother pulled him back
while Father stood there paralyzed.

The death dealer returned
and once more pulled out young "every other."
Again Mother pulled him back
and slapped the guard
who shot her on the spot
leaving the fourteen-year-old
on the line of life.

LITTLE MOSHE

Little Moshe cries.
I change him.
An ugly rash!
I should have changed him
Two hours ago
In memory of
A thousand little Moshes
Whose mothers went out for milk
In their slippers
And never came back
A million little Moshes
Who cried out their souls
From open sores on their tender bottoms.

TWO BUS RIDES

Round the corner careens
This rickety old bus
Flattened leather seats
Worn to high shine
Twenty years of wide bottoms
Up, down, all day long
Except on Shabbat.

Tightly I clutch my strap
Lest I fall sideways
Into a stranger's lap
Though there's no stranger here
For everyone's jabbering
About everyone's business.

Gold haze turns to gray
Against the Jerusalem stone
As we grind gears
Up this narrow street
Suddenly silence
Our curly-haired driver
With tan muscled arms
Plaid sleeves tightly rolled
Stops chewing his gum
And raises the volume
As every neck strains
"Kol Yisrael Shalom"
Greets a manicured voice
"The hour is seven"
Economic jam first
A good sign, a great blessing
No disasters today
Not a single son lost.

The Geneva bus
That I rode last week
Was near perfect and new
Routinely replaced
To be silent not gaseous
With unscratched enamel
And clean plastic fittings
Took corners so smoothly
Slid gently downhill
Not a creak could be heard
So passengers whisper
If they talk at all
These perfect bystanders
With fresh Alpine skins
Cool uniformed driver
Xenophobically pleasant
Calls out my stop
Route de Ferney.

Why cannot Egged
Buy a new bus?

Well, we did not bank
Bars, bars of gold teeth
From unwilling mouths
And we did not keep
Great numbered accounts
With every heir gone.

SECOND LIFE

Mr. S. celebrates his daughter's birthday
He is sixty, she twelve
I wonder if he is thinking
About that little girl
Whose picture I saw
In their hallway
Sweet face, curly hair all over her head
Shining, giving off shafts of light
Expensive frilly dress
A very small picture
Tucked into a corner
Of the hallway wall
Was that her birthday picture?
I hope he cannot read my thoughts
Nor I his
As he celebrates this happy family day
In his second life.

THE CHAZZAN FROM TARNOPOL

Henry's voice
Crackled at the edges
No longer did it satisfy, serve,
Lift, uplift,
Carry the congregation.

Still
He stood throughout the *tefillah*
In the corner of his pew
In the glass and cedar
Angled ceiling
Sunlit, red-carpeted
Design-award-winning
Shul in northern New Jersey
"Another Bergen"
He laughed
With his brother.

"Why stand, Henry?"
His elegant, Chanel-suited wife pleaded
(In another life
She would have
Called him Chaimke
But here, now,
In this Lincoln Continental
Glass and cedar crowd
Henry must do.)

"No longer the chazzan"
She railed
"Varicose veins . . ."

"Embarrasses the rabbi . . ."
("Embarrasses me," she means)
"So stubborn, my Henry"
She told "the girls"
With a transparent laugh.

"When I sit I'll die"
He had confided long ago
In a darkened room
In an intimate moment.

As his friends raced
Speedily toward death
While standing in aching stillness
At five-hour roll call
Chaimke transformed himself
Into the chazzan of Tarnopol
Descendant of a long line
Of illustrious sweet singers of Israel
"*Ehrliche chazzunim*"
He lovingly called them.

While the men of Tarnopol
Stepped outside for a shmooze
And a breath of air
And the women of Tarnopol
Rushed home
To feed the young
Fasting till noon
Chaimke stood without respite
On aching legs
From morning till night
From *shacharis* and *musaf*

To *minchah* and *neilah*
With a stomach that rumbled
And lips that parched
Growing stronger each moment
Feeling life restored
As he pleaded with God
This stubborn
Messenger of the congregation.

"When I sit, I'll die."
Long ago
In that darkened room
She understood.

LOVE

How lucky we are
To have this time.

Once, I read in *Life*
That husbands and wives
In Chinese communes
Could make love
On Saturday nights only
In special huts
For fifteen minutes
While couples waited outside
In long lines.

How lucky we are
How luxurious
A whole hour
A whole night.

Once, I read in a diary
That one Esther,
Married in a bunker,
Never even had fifteen minutes.
When her new husband returned
Through the sewers that morning
He found them all gone.

A NEW HAIR STYLE

A girl named Goody
I love her so.

I see her
Fleetingly
As I pass
Through the living room
A glimpse, a gift
Not knowing
She'd be there.

Slender arms
Little pointed chin
Deep brown hair
Good strong bones
Long graceful neck.
"Perhaps you'll be
A ballet dancer
With that long neck"
I said to her
When she was eight.
"How can you dance
With your neck?"
She laughed
And then
Freely danced
With her neck.

Today, cross-legged
On the sofa
She sports
A new hair style

Plain, pleasant,
Parted to the side
With a small white barrette
In the shape
Of a bow.
"How do you like it?"
She bubbles.
"Pretty," I say,
"Very pretty"
Though inside
A stab
As the face
On the cover
Of a diary
Flashes before me
A bright gay spirit
A bursting spirit
Contained
In one crowded room
Cut off
In one more crowded.

Is that why
I love you so tonight,
My Goody?

THE BEETLE

Winter of '73:
A clearness in the air
Born of cold
Icy glistening cold
A clear
So clear
So pure
Clouded only
By the immediate mist
Spun of a labored exhale.
I should have worn my black suede boots
He should have left me the car.

The bus is long in coming
I'll be late for class
At seven past nine
The students will bolt
With glee
Having done their part.

A horn sounds
It must be Elijah
"Hey. Mrs. G.
Wanna ride?"
Kevin
Sophomore or junior . . . I forget
Blue eyes, freckles
Easy, winning smile
That will drive some
Katherine or Peggy wild.
Kevin, C + on the midterm
Kevin, nice guy.

"Thanks, Kevin
Now we'll *both* be on time"
Not that funny
But student and teacher laugh
Enjoying a moment's camaraderie
That crosses lines and
Makes me feel younger.

"New car?"
"Yup, a week old
Nineteenth birthday. . ."
(So the Irish, too
Are upwardly mobile)
"Thirty-two m.p.g.
In city traffic
Handles great
Almost parks itself.
Neat little job."

We laugh again

But I must
Twist the knife
My Christian friend
Softly, very softly
"Too bad it's German-made
I could never buy one."

A long silence
Irritation?
Exasperation?
"Jeez, Mrs. G.
How long you gonna remember?"

In my heart
I answer
Until I die, Kevin
Until you die, Kevin
Until the whole world dies.

Too bad!
In the next cold rain
Kevin will probably
Pass me by
That lachrymose Jewish teacher.

WHAT A MIRACLE!

Of all my loves
Of *yiddishkeit*
I'll choose
Shabbat
Shiva
Brachot

Macht a bruchah
Sweet, sweet
Words of love
For everything

Wine
  borei pri hagafen
New trees
  shelo chisar beolamo . . .
Circumcision
  bivrito shel avraham avinu
Rainbow
  zocher habrit . . .
Apricot nectar
  shehakol nihyeh bidvaro
Torah reading
  asher bachar banu . . .
Purple cashmere
  malbish arumim
Candles
  lehadlik ner. . .
Sitting in the sukkah
  leysheyv basukkah
A wise man
  shenatan mechachmato. . .

Urination
  asher yatzar . . .
Miraculous saving
  hagomel lechayavim tovot . . .

Did Daniel ever
Recite *hagomel*
From forty-three to forty-five?
Hunted, starved.
Whipped, betrayed
Each one a miracle
That saved his life

Macht a bruchah
Daniel

Does God suffer
Daniel's *brachah?*

ELEH EZKERAH

On my way to shul Yom Kippur morning
I pass a cherry-picker
Trimming a lavish tree
Feeding its chopped limbs
Into the masher
To clear the wires
And lighten the street.

On my way to shul Yom Kippur morning
To recite *eleh ezkerah*
I hear the gears grinding
I remember Rabban Shimon
Whose head they sliced off;
I remember Rabbi Akiva
Body combed with iron;
I remember Rabbi Chananya
Burnt, wrapped in a drenched Torah.

I remember them all
And the artist of Terezin
Whose hand they chopped off
For painting scenes
Of his brothers' woe.

Not even for selling
His brother
For a pair of sandals.

MY NEIGHBORS

The Benders are my neighbors
In a new apartment building
In Manhattan
Low ceilings, white walls,
Modern kitchens.
Our first bond, Sabbath observance
And the men's *kippot.*
Our second, the children,
My three little ones whom she adores
They go to her apartment
For Paula's cookies, gum,
Hugs, and kisses.

He is always sick
With bad lungs
She cares for him like a mother
Although she is his niece.
After the war
They found each other
Two left of a large family.
So they married
In the D.P. camp.

He complains.
Sometimes I think to myself
He is spoiled, immature
More like a child
Than an uncle-husband
She tries to ease
His discomfort
His congested lung.

About herself, she never complains
Never
Only once
To whisper quickly
That she has
No children
Because of the experiments.

KINDERGARTEN, THE BRONX

Fives and sixes
And a four-year-old pushed ahead
Innocent young things
Beginnings of a pack.

Suzie, home from school
"Look, mom, I can hop"
As she hops
To the kitchen table
For a snack and rerun
Of kindergarten intrigue.

"Mom," says the little voice
With a milk moustache
And pink-ribboned ponytails
"What does ant mean?"
"A tiny bug
That crawls in the dirt,"
Says mom smartly
Small knot of fear
Tightening in her belly
"No, Aunt is a lady
Tammy has Aunt Judy
And Michael . . . and Lauren . . .
Do I have an Aunt?"
"No," says mom
Sensing her neat charade
Is now in danger
"Why not?"

The beribboned ponytails
Press relentlessly forward.

Three aunts
And
The beginning
Of the end
Of Innocence.

STOMACH VIRUS

I feel sick.
The flu, the virus
Aches, cramps, nausea.
Alice takes carpool.
I cancel my class.

A nice clean bathroom
Off my bedroom
Ivory fixtures and tiles
Aztec print paper
Vacant all day.
Blessed temporary relief
Until the next round.
Back to a warm bed
To sleep a few more hours.

Y. comes home early to feed the children.
Tomorrow I'll make up car pool.
My students will be waiting for me.

There, dysentery spelled death.
Still I curse my rotten luck
At each new round of pain.

A BLUE PANTS SUIT

A march for Soviet Jews
Spring, 1974
I walk behind Mrs. R.
She wears a powder-blue pants suit
And I know why.

At the very end,
The death march from Auschwitz
She, mother, and sister escaped.
When they heard the German tanks,
Also fleeing,
They hid in a ditch.
One sadist,
Your average, decent German
Spotted three Jewish women
Cowering in the ditch.
Smoothly
He detoured his tank
To run them over.
Toward evening
The mother died
After holding out for so long.
Both sisters' legs were crushed.

Mrs. R. once said to me
"I love pants suits"
But her neighbor
Told me the rest.

HONEY, I SAID

"Honey,"
I said, trying
to modulate the inflection
so as to convey
nonchalance
(though after all these years
I still don't know
how to feign that
instead of vexation
or impatience
which I know
irritates the hell out of him
when it comes to
my commenting on
[criticizing, let's be honest]
the way he dresses
or won't try new foods
or makes a social gaffe
from too much honesty
his trademark)
"pull your collar out in back"
so it won't show
an unsightly bulge
at the rib
under the gorgeous, soft
gray cashmere V neck pullover
that I bought for him
a gift for no occasion
no design at all
but love.

He's four steps down
the open staircase

of this split level
summer home
on a cool August morning
with its premature feel of Fall
attacking my knee.
He's reading
and I'm wondering why
he gets so rankled
takes it so personally
when I'm rather grateful
if he tells me
my slip is showing
or I've put on too much blush
or gently hints
that the print is unflattering
or I shouldn't have said this
to that one
or a thousand and one things
that husbands and wives
teach, cover, finesse
remonstrate, caution, edit
criticize, second guess
each other
all signs
that I care
my beloved's keeper.

Order a salad
(against colon cancer)
Get to bed early
(so you won't look haggard at
the board meeting)
Take on that freebie lecture

(it's good exposure)
Call the mourners overseas
(They're big donors)
Prepare the token now
(so as not to fish under your
overcoat at the bridge toll)
And don't meet the world today
with a hump at the nape of your neck.

He's standing on the steps
reading the mail and not paying attention.
So,
I go over
and matter of factly
without fanfare
standing two steps above him
reach over and
insert my finger
under the back
of his shirt collar
and gently (I think) lift it up and out
over the sweater
casually reading
over his shoulder
an old pattern
that
he doesn't mind.

It's Hanna Hirshaut
in Emunah Women's *Lest We Forget**
remembering
_____

* Hanna Hirschaut's memoir was first published in *Martyrdom and Resistance*, 1979, and reprinted in *Lest We Forget*, June, 1993.

that stifling hot day
at the gates
near the Umschlagplatz
fifty years ago
watching her kid sister
from the hidden window
overlooking the plaza.

Yesterday, Hanna and five others
old girlfriends
a renegade band of 18 year olds
who gambled on nothing to lose
made plans to defy
the order
and wedged themselves
into a second story concealed room
near the roundup
where the dogs wouldn't notice.

Yesterday, Hanna had tried
But the 15 year old said no.

I watched her in the blazing sun
so beautiful
so fragile
herded.

The image scorches.
The fight is gone out of me.
So what does it matter
a shirt collar bunched up under
a sweater neckline
this cool August morning?

"SOPHIE'S CHOICE"

Years ago, the question of names
Had consumed Sophie
With but one filled
By Blossom, pride and joy
Only child of an only living child
Called, after Sophie's mother
Blimeleh.

Years ago, Sophie would lie awake
Anxiously awaiting Blossom
To be safely inside
By midnight and then 1:00 a.m. curfew
After a pristine date with a suited male.

Waiting, she'd fill her mind
With images of years ahead
Of infants and toddlers
And sweet-smelling new life.
Every Wednesday Sophie would leave
Their candy store on De Kalb
And take the subway
To Bensonhurst or Flatbush
Or Far Rockaway?
In each hand, a shopping bag
Of glass and plastic, filled to the brim
With gefilte fish and noodle pudding
Fresh-baked cookies with tiny currants
Instead of raisins and nuts
And soft meatballs in tomato sauce
With no bones for the little ones.
To Blossom's house she'd travel
To a street with trees and side yards

To give her only child
A helping hand
Free time for errand runs
A day on the town
A chance to restore strength, recover self
After nursing and nurturing
A gaggle of children
Just as Sophie knew
Mama would have done for her
In baby Blossom's years.

Years ago, the question would intrude sweet fantasy
Whose name to give first, after papa's?
Whose name, of five sisters
Older and younger than she
Elke, the oldest,
Or Bryna, the third.
Sophie's dearest friend and
Most grievous loss
After mama.
Or Ruchel, the baby
Who never reached womanhood.
Which to give first, and second,
And who might have no name?
Again pain
Of selection.

And what if only boys there'd be?
Could Elke become Elchanan?
Or Ruchel Ralph?
And she laughed aloud in bed
So that her husband startled awake
"Is Blossom home?"

And promptly fell back asleep
Knowing Sophie worried enough
For both of them.

But now she lay awake
Bereft of questions
For Blossom's pristine womb
Was shrinking
And her practice expanding
The clock ticking away
And no man in sight.

No choice. The end
Of Reb Elimelech's line.

SAFETY STATISTICS

For all peoples
Of this century
The likelihood
Of dying on a train
Is significantly lower
With small margin of error
Than in a car, bus, boat, or plane
Except for Jews

BEACH DAY

We are
Crowded
Hot
Uncomfortable
In the wagon
Three adults, five children
Traffic at a dead standstill
All of New York
Coming home from the beach,
All of New York
Westbound on the L.I.E.
Why didn't we spend that
Three hundred on air-conditioning!

"I can't wait!" says J.J.
"Hold it in."
"I can't." he cries.
We open the car door slightly
The kids laugh at how the baking highway
Sends up a steaming vapor from J.J.'s water.

Minutes later, three kids are fighting.
Feeling locked in,
I rail at all of them
Even the two who are laughing, not fighting.

I roar, though
Five minutes ago,
The thought passed
In and out
In an instant

For twenty
Thirty
Forty
Hours
No door opened
No air-conditioner hummed.

And after all
J.J. only had to . . .

A DINNER PARTY

Pink damask cloth, artichoke hearts
Candlelight, a long dress

I say blithely
To the man next to me,
"In prison for three days?
How terrible!
How could you stand it?"
The words slipped out
Could not be recalled
Nor could I then say to him,
"Maidanek for three years?
How terrible!
How could you stand it?"

I hope no one noticed
My watery eyes
Which cleared even before
We laughed
At the end line of some
Clever dinner-party tale.

THE RAV

Grown men in new double breasted Pesach suits
Weeping softly into salt and pepper beards
Sniffling sorrowfully into hand rolled, white polyester hand-
kerchiefs
Weeping but not wailing, for Parkinson's plague
Throbbed away his last decade
Preparing the day, softening the blow
Beloved teacher ever protecting his charges
But now the floodgates have opened
Memories surging, pulsing, crowding in
Each man a story, each man a child.

Brysker genius, mellifluous poet-philosopher
Bridger of tradition and modernity
Lonely man of faith
Creator of leaders
He sucked the marrow of halacha
And left it nourished.

How rich we were
to have him
to be the generation
that adored him
revered, honored,
cherished, appreciated
held him in awe
to be the students
who loved him
thirsted after every word
repeated his Torah
feared his questions
sought his blessing

craved his approbation
warmed under his praise
to be the rabbis
who treasured him
felt him as a father
quoted him in our sermons
phoned him with our *shaiylos*
visited him in Onset
called him Rebbe
to be the community
that followed him
named him our leader
pored over his writings
synthesized this with that
educated our women
created our Unions
called ourselves "modern"

At 90 he left us
Bereft
He was one in a million
An *illui*, a young genius
Gadol hador
All said it was so

He came here in '32.
Were there five others?

TRUTH AND LIES IN A SUBWAY CAR

I ask
but he tells me
he never really "found out"
it was imbibed with his mother's milk
though, like other modern
mothers of the fifties, she nursed him
not a single moment.
A sigh a day
a story a week
in that household
and two or five when the friends came
no matter the *shah shahs*
Shush,
Sh, Sh
around a doe-eyed little boy.

But Sarah's daughter found out
one ordinary day
in an old, 60's subway car
rocking her noisily to Erasmus High.
The single wide khaki door
slides open right to left
enters a petite woman
eyes her, catches her breath
recognition coming.
In an accent thick
as the old brown
leather suitcase she carries
"You must be Sarah's daughter,
image of her at your age."

Talking, cautiously
for this was plainly no stranger

as in a mother's thousand times
Don't talk to . . . .

"Together a year
in Lager B
where is she now?"

"That's not my mom
She was safe."
The woman gasps
exits at the next stop
never to be heard from again

After school
After bio, typing, boys
algebra, new saddles,
civics, the girls, cracking gum
Sarah's daughter puts
her key in the lock
and calls out
in a voice different
from all the yesterdays
"Mom? Mom?"

The stranger shouldn't have run
for the girl had known
all these years
it was a pack of lies
and now there was
one more loss.

REVERSE LEVIR

And so he says
　Leaning forward
　　On his hard wooden stool
　　My soft-spoken
　　　Dry cleaner
　　　Who works
　　　　From eight to eight
　　　　Sitting now beside
　　　　　His slippered brother
　　　　　Who listens knowingly
　　　　　To old family lore
　　　　　Their eyes
　　　　　Dry

"As we were leaving
　For the forest
　　Melech's young wife
　　I remember her now
　　Shy and beautiful
　　　Changed her mind
　　　Would not give up
　　　Their child"

"If you survive
　She said
　　Maybe you'll stay
　　In the family
　　And consider
　　My sister
　　　So my little brother
　　　Married his wife's sister

They lived together
　　Forty years
　　　　Fourteen grandchildren"

As they sit there
　On wooden stools
　　Sitting *shiva*
　　　For the first
　　　Time and
　　　　For the whole
　　　　　Family (the others
　　　　All went in one
　　　　Year, unnoted)
　　　　I wonder,
　　　　　Did Melech and
　　　　　　His second bride
　　　　　Cry in bed
　　　　　　When they made
　　　　　Love? Did all
　　　　　　Fresh *yevamot*?
　　　　　If not
　　　　　　Then how . . .

Tonight in bed
　I shall weep
　　For that first bride.

FAST FOOD

What good fortune
A job!

A clean uniform
Comforting red and white striped
With matching hat
Perky young people
Plump and dimpled blondes
And sassy slick haired men
Coming on to a newcomer
In words only
Ah, the good old days.
Two twenty four minimum wage
The American dream

Scrub the counters
Sweep the stone floor
Wash the greasy linoleum
Of a frying kitchen
Empty the ketchup splattered trays
Don the hat
And serve burgers, fries and coke
Wretchedly *treyf*
But never mind
It pays the rent
Of a sunless cold water flat
Whose night is memories
And day is dreams

But the sleeve hits the elbow
And the blue eyed dimpled blonde
Spots the numbers and says Impossible

You must have been a criminal
Or something

Lock up the story
And throw away the key
And smile at the sassy young men's flirt

TRIGGER WORDS

Action
Barking
Boots
Butterfly
Bystander
Cattle car
Chamber
Chosen
Collaborate
Drek
Dysentery
Experiments
Eye sockets
Forests
Gold teeth
Lampshade
Latrine
Orchestra
Soap
Solution
Swine
Transport
Wheelbarrow
Yellow
God

TWENTIETH-CENTURY RIDDLE

Who is older than her mother
Older than her grandmothers?

Answer:
Lydia.
Auburn hair
With gray-brown roots
Wide green eyes
Framed by soft crow's-feet
Fine skin
With a wrinkle or two
As befits a matron
Of fifty-seven.

Lydia
Remembers her mother
Fair, creamy complexion
Air-brushed by the years
Wearing a big white hat on Shavuot
The fur boa
A young girl nestled against
On winter outings
Beautiful mama
Young enough
In the mind's eye
To be her daughter.

Lydia
Remembers the grandmothers
Nagymama Sosha and Bubbe Clara
Two elegant Hungarian ladies

Gabor style
Wearing white gloves and red veils
Lunching in cafes
Taking her to the park
With her big brother of ten
(Ah, where is he now?)

The grandmothers made jam for Pesach
Stuffed cabbage for papa
They painted their nails
And Lydia's, too
She played
In the lace-curtained parlor
Napped in their high beds
Rummaged musical jewelry boxes
Fingered the mirrored tray
Crowded with lotions and creams
Not a line in their faces
Skins fine, luminescent
Two elegant Hungarian grandmas
Who died without a wrinkle.

They all said a hurried good-bye
On a cloudless Budapest day, 1944
Lydia, in her Shavuot dress
Taken by nagymama's stout cook
Her brother, sent off to a farmer
Never heard from again.

"*Emlékezz*, " said beautiful mama
After the last "Be a good girl"
And final hugs
"*Emlékezz*"

Remember
"Te egy zsidó vágy
*Drága lányom."**
But tell no one.

Who is older than her own mother?
Older than the world?

A twentieth-century riddle.

_____

* You are a Jew, my dear daughter.

You are cordially invited

to the dedication of the

Restored Sefer Torah

Lithuanian Courtyard

Martyrs' Remembrance

Valley of Destroyed Communities

Second-Generation Conference

Righteous-Gentile Awards

Reinterment of Family Bones

Bergen-Belsen Survivors' Ball

Leaders' Trip to Auschwitz

Kristallnacht Services

Opening of the Boxcar Memorial

Gathering of the Hidden Children

TIME

Oh, how much Jewish time
And energy
From now unto
The nth generation.

MAY 14TH: AN OLD PRIESTESS, A NEW PRIESTESS

Click—wind forward—click
Here they come
Sunny marchers
Of fifth grade
Two laughing priestesses
Arm in arm
As Jaffa oranges
With green leaves
Of oaktag
And crepe paper
Tribute to our
Independence

Mine, the blonde
Descends from Aaron
Ablutions, sacrifices
Goats of Azazel
And welcome tithes
She ends a line
Muted once
By Temple razed
Cut forever
By female chromosomes

Her little friend
With topaz eyes
Is first
Of the new line
With no gender gap

It begins with destruction
Ablutions by fire
Human scapegoats
Outnumbering the remnant
Atonement for God
Welts over old scars
A child torn away
One left of hundreds

My Deborah will tell
Her grandchildren
As they sprawl
On her carpet
Inquiring
Of old photos
I once knew
A girl whose
Mother
And
Father
Survived that other planet
Come here and touch me

HER NEIGHBORS DON'T KNOW

Yonkers is all ado
But not about nothing
Low-income housing that
"Ruins neighborhoods"
"Keep out the 'others'"
"Good apples" and
"Rotten ones."

On Bryant Lane
In her small, two-story
Red-brick bungalow
(Hall bannister shiny
From pulling herself up
Hand over hand
Basement apartment rented
Earth level supporting her)
Lives a tiny ageless woman
Sea-blue eyes
Neatly laced, high-arched
Polished-black, old-lady shoes.

Fourscore years ago
She fell from
A Ukrainian tree
Doll in hand
Her mother carried her
On her arms
Three days and nights
Praying to Mary alone
So life was spared
With a humpback
And no beaus

For endless teens
Her neighbors don't know.

At seventeen
Crossing dart-eyed
Into the ghetto
To give school-chum Bluma
Pumpernickel
From the "other side"
A shiny bullet
Grazed Janka's knee
Her neighbors don't know.

(Was it her hump?
"For you were strangers . . ."
Yet . . . .
Trocmé's wife
Le Chambon's first lady
Was a straight-backed beauty.)

Her brother-in-law
Was kept unaware
That mother and she
Hid four Jews
In their attic
For two years
A scare a day.

One fine morning
As the Nazis gleefully
Came upon fanned aces
And fresh ashes
Her fast-talking

Nephew of nine
Begged them
Not to tell
"Mama will kill me
If she hears
I was up here
Smoking and playing cards
With my friends"
While four terrorized Jews
Panted underground.

Janka of Yonkers
Should wear golden slippers
And be drawn in a carriage
By silky white horses
And the quick-witted lad
Now a father in the Ukraine
Should own a hundred shares
Of Olympia and York
And their neighbors should know.

SYMBOLS OF LIFE

In every culture
So they say
Eggs
White or brown
Symbolize
The round of life
Endless life.

So, serve them whole
At a mourner's first meal
Or deviled
At a happy *bris*
Or with ashes
Before Tisha B'Av
Or saltwater dipped
At a family seder
Or chopped with raw onions
At a singing *shalleshudos*
Or garnished
At a *simchat bat*.

Does Riva remember
As she slices eggs
For the feast
Of covenanting
Her new granddaughter
How she fell
At age fifteen
Under her mother's
Crumpling, innocent body
Shot by the S.S.
Because mama

Moved her hand
To hide her crime
In the cupboard
One extra egg
Over the ration
A mother dead
For the crime
Of one extra
Round of life?

POLISH ASYLUMS

Warsaw's Bellevue is closed
So they're out on the streets
A few crazy old ladies
With matted hair
And glassy eyes
And rocking arms
Waiting at the station
For their babies to come home.

WEDDING-LIST QUOTA

'What's your cutoff point?"
Inquires Aunt Dora
"Through first cousins"
"Good, then Milton . . .
A new production . . .
Coming East in June . . ."

"Great," as I roll my eyes
Secretly in my skull
For I do love Milt
Though it's been six years
And wrote his name
On the Not Coming list
A month before
The invites were mailed
And added
One more friend

Fifty-nine cousins
Half our limit
My mother one of seven
My father one of six
All straight, square
With old family values
Thank God, Yitz has a small family

Good God, bite my tongue!
One hundred cousins
From Lodz, Siedlce, Lomza, Vilna.

ALL IN ONE

In a black and white photo
Against a flat stone wall
I glimpsed her wearing it
Boned body garment
We used to call all-in-one
That tucked us in so shapely
And it bolted off the wall
And tore into my heart
Where it will not leave
For a month of Sundays
And a thousand color snapshots
Of adorable children at the beach

She was running through the streets
Of Lvov where
Better men who ate on dowry *kest*
Had hunched
Day and night over tractates
And did not squander their thoughts on
How beautiful is this tree

Running, with one strap fallen
A brown nipple showing
Garters hugging solid thighs
That would sag
Next month
If she were lucky
Running, with a pack of aghast women
A helmeted 12 year old
With shotgun in splay position
Laughing alongside, reveling in early manhood
Running, hairpins loosening, strands flying

Upswept hairdo coming undone
Like the grand life
That ended twenty minutes ago

ROMEO AND JULIET

But they saw him at Auschwitz
And he never came out
So she waited nine months
And dreamed of him every night
Then married a landsman
And had two children
But six years later
He came back to life
Victims again
All

DOMESTIC HELP

Domestic help is a bargain
If you speak their language
If not, talk slowly and loudly
Laugh and point.
Danuta cared for Grandma
So gently I forgot
Her origins in one day
And she stayed till Grandma died.
My dear friend Manya has
Gone through four Danutas
In two years
Though she speaks
Their language in soft tones
Working out numbered years
And a single moment
At the corner bakery
In Lublin at war's end
Home to find,
Please God, even one
Who fell through the net.

At the counter
Stood her neighbor's daughter
Wearing for sure
Mama's fur coat.
Upon inquiry
The furred bitch screamed
"Hitler should have finished off all of you"
And the baker's wife
Stood silent
Again.

BINDINGS

Sydney, 1992

Oh beautiful down under
Of shimmering lakes and green lushness
Aborigines and immigrants
Deputies and Crocodile Dundees
Rock bands, opera sails
Koalas, kangaroos and Queensland coral

And a synagogue newly built
By the biggest builder in town
Who etched into the concrete facade
A single pair of tefillin, his father's treasure
Instead of golden lions and cherubs
Six pointed stars, seven branched menorahs
Or stained glass tribes
The first of its kind in aboriginal history

Palm Springs, 1991

Standing in the lobby shop
Of the "kosher le Pesach" hotel
Waiting for the Times, set aside
During the "first days" of no money exchanged
Sydney's native son
Builder's son
First generation Peter
Hears an accented voice ahead of him
Requesting *his* paper.
But there's no imposter here
For these strangers share a last name

99

And they talk, standing

Under fluorescent lights, amidst passersby,
People and stuffed palm trees
The forty-seven year mystery is finally solved:
What happened to Peter's grandfather
Last seen on Monday morning, March 20th, 1944
When the young father of six
Hurried off to the main train station
To buy tickets
To take the family back to Fulek
Out of harm's way

We were rounded up together at the station
Six weeks in a holding pen
Then shipped off.
Leaving the transport
Ordered to leave all possessions
But that loving Jew from Fulek
Returned to the pile
To take back his little bag
And didn't survive the beating
The guard knifed open the worn velvet
To find a Jew's treasure

I always wanted to tell someone

Heart of man
Eternal covenant
Pesach in Palm Springs
Tefillin in concrete
Who can fathom it?

THIS WAY TO THE SHOWERS

Adjusting the spray to prickly
Regulating the temperature to a perfect warm-hot
Soaping the sponge with Caswell-Massey Jasmine
Lathering my skin with silky, white bubbles
Shampooing my hair with Nexxus II
Resetting my oil glands, great luxury of life

Will I ever
Be able to
Just shower?

A PLEASURE TO INTRODUCE

Laureate, leader, artist, activist.
Fearless, peerless. . .

The intros
Are always long
For he did so much
For so many

The intros
Are always grand
For he is a man
Of rare talents

The intros
Are always painful
When they get to hero
All he ever hears
For forty years
From that moment he stepped
Into the sewer
Leading the young and strong
Is his old mother's wail
Don't leave me behind

WHAT WOULD I HAVE DONE?

This time I'm lying in bed
thinking about nothing
in particular
and the old nightmare returns
(or is it connected
to the sea adventure
we watched two hours ago?)
and the boatman tells me
I can take only one with me
decide now for we're shoving off
and I'm holding Deborah
and the boys are clinging
to my skirt

This time I'm walking along
a Crown Heights street
and the elderly couple
ahead of me are walking together
though not exactly
for she's a constant
three inches behind him
and they pull his head back
by his hair
forcing him to open his eyes
as one straddles his wife
the modest rebbetzin
another, his virgin daughter
who says Papa don't cry
it doesn't hurt

This time I'm passing through
a tiny Swiss village

and the high speed train
from Lucerne to Zurich's airport
doesn't even bother to stop
and the stationmaster nods along on his chest
and the notice posted on the station house
threatens anyone caught harboring a Jew swine
with execution in the public square
along with his entire household
guarding the secret
should I buy extra bread for them today?

This time I'm reading
a men's fashion retrospective
of the gay 20's
those liberating bathing suits
you know, the black and white
one piece jerseys
on fine boned men
with cute behinds
and the fat and hated beast
who wears and gives stripes
wants her
and will give her kid sister
a lighter work load
but can you die here with dignity anyhow?

What would I . . .

TOOLS OF WAR

Sharpened knife
Glinting in the light
Steel clamp
Dull and cold
Drawn blood
Drops of wine
Sucked through the lips
To still the screams

Today
We have gone to battle
In full dress
The entire force
Clamoring
Then silent
Called up
On Shabbat
A holy war
Emerging
Victorious

TOOLS OF WAR II

Light streams through
The huge glass pane
Beaded with glistening droplets
A tree framed in its center
By the architect and his Master Partner
Rays catching the glowing olive-wood ark
Embroidered threads of Elijah's chair
Gray-black strands of the *mohel*'s beard
Shiny white teeth of a two-year-old "big" brother
Held against his mother's softened, still rounded belly
Grandmother's silk dress and wedding pearls
The *sandek's* sparkling old blue eyes.

We rise.
Baruch ata
A swift cut
A drop of blood
A tiny fierce cry
Silenced with sweet wine
Baruch ata
Nissan Chayyim
Miracle of life in the first month
Shouts of joy
For Torah, canopy, good deeds
Enter our covenant
Eighth-day prince held aloft
To oohs and aahs
And self-congratulations
For he is now all ours
We have won
Another victory.

TOOLS OF WAR—POSTSCRIPT

Oh, we have won
Another victory

Or have we added
One more hostage?

RESISTING YOM HASHOAH, 1985

A purple crocus thrusts up
Near the ancient oak
The mourning dove coos
Its velvety call
As the street comes alive
With the tinny beep
Of car-pool caravans
Carrying gay young children
To their refreshed teachers

Dawn's dew dampens
The rolled and rubber-banded *Times*
Tossed from a speeding van
Onto the greening grass
A blue-crowned jay
Glides from oak to mulberry to maple
In surprising silence

No matter.
I hear the song
In my heart
This fresh spring morning
Dreamt of months ago
In January's bone-chilling grayness

Morning's work becomes a blessing
All cliches are true
Good to be alive
Healthy, safe, loving, working
The ink flows, the pen chases
Its shadow across the page

Seldom does the phone ring
Interrupting thought
Few the descents
To the refrigerator
My spirits soar
Then level
Then soar once more
It is a day
For which women who write
In their homes
Are born

Midday, the spring sun
Moves forward and backward
Slipping in and out
Of feathery clouds
Midday, and a speck of gloom
Barely noticed
Settles round the joyous edges
Spreading slowly
As the seconds race
Toward the newly sacred day
That will begin at dusk

Late afternoon
Like a spreading stain
The heaviness
Creeps unwelcome
Toward the heart's lining
Not yet piercing
Yet not unknown

I long to hold the lightness

Lengthen the cheer
One moment more
But I cannot
Soon I will be overtaken
By memory's pain
My people's woe

Now anger lurches in
Fury and rage explode
Why must I give them
Victory anew
The laughing tormentors
Who rise in their graves
To assault my calendar?
Why must I pay
An eve of sadness
Limbs weighted down
By close horror
That sharpens with time?
No, I shall not go
No heartbreak for me tonight
No one will pummel my spirits
Not tonight
No!

Seven-thirty
Time for *maariv*
And I leave for Loehmann's
Faintly excusing myself with
"I remember all year long"
"Good girl, I've always gone"
Tonight no one is home
To chastise

To raise an eyebrow
As I drive away
From the setting sun
The song cranks up again
Slightly off-tune
And fighting for space
Inside the lining
Tonight at Loehmann's I shall find
A beautiful dress
A party dress
A Yom Hashoah victory dress
I laugh perversely
Sweeping through the racks
I load my aching arms
For the journey
To the try-on room
Where a darting-eyed salesgirl
With fresh pimples calls out
"Only six garments at a time"
"Over the head, ladies"

Tonight only a few wigged women
From Boro Park
Have trekked to Loehmann's Bronx
Among them Hungarians
Who ache all year long
Amid silver and crystal
But brook no change
In Sinai's calendar

In time, I find it
A beautiful Norma Kamali
This season's colors

Yellow and black
No matter
I shall wear it

At nine, the intercom vibrates
The assistant manager's staccato voice
With a hint of desperation
After ten hours on her feet
Enmeshed in fabrics, hangers, racks
Half-naked ladies
Cash registers that bleep
Instead of ring
Harsh fluorescent lights
Mindless, gossipy packers
"This store is closing
In thirty minutes
Please take your final solutions
To the cash register"

Giving up the ghost
I fling Norma Kamali
Yellow and black
Over the rack
And rush out

I reach shul
Just as the faithful
Half of them survivors
Purged once more
Begin to file out
Dispersing sooner than usual
A few linger
Somber and subdued

On the concrete plaza
Beneath the street light
A few laugh, softly, self-consciously

I sit in my car
Across the street
Until the last soul has departed
Knowing
This is where I belong

MY WAY

I am the princess on the pea
That's the way I'm going to be
Creature comforts all for me
Like my chaise longue by the sea

"Ooh, it's raining, hail a cab"
"Stop! I must cotton this toenail scab"
"Radio's loud, shut off that blab"
"Candlelight dinner, you pay the tab"

"Please don't interrupt, I've a deadline to meet"
"Order by phone, I can't stand on my feet"
"Air-condition this hot, hot suite"
"Ah, it's time for my persimmon treat"

"Off I go to visit my mother"
"This shop is not stocked, let's go find another"
"I'm busy now, kids, go ask your father"
"If the trip is too long, I simply won't bother"

"This elastic waist's a bit too tight"
"Open the shades. I need more light"
"Fax it to me, I want it tonight"
"Let's pay the fine and avoid a fight"

"I'm feeling tired, I'll take a nap"
"Come sweet child, sit in my lap"
"I'll have spring water, it's better than tap"
"It's chilly in here, please fetch my wrap"

"Get the best seats at the new play"
"Porter, come carry this suitcase away"
"I wish to have it done my way"

I'd not have survived a single day.

GLOSSARY*

Al kiddush hashem—Death as a martyr; also an ethical act that reflects honor on the Jewish people and Judaism.

Asher bachar banu—The blessing that speaks of God's choosing the Jewish people and giving them the Torah.

Asher Yatzar—The blessing recited after bodily elimination, praising God for the wondrous ways the body functions.

Badeken—*(Yiddish)* The ceremony immediately prior to a Jewish wedding during which the groom gently draws the wedding veil over the bride's face.

Baruch ata—"Blessed are You": opening words of most blessings.

Bentsh—*(Yiddish)* "Bless." Refers here to reciting the Grace after meals.

Bivrito shel Avraham avinu—Blessing recited by a father upon the circumcision of his son.

Borei pri hagafen—Blessing recited over wine.

Brachah—*pl.* **brachos, brachot**—Blessing.

Bris, Brit—Covenant; circumcision ceremony performed on an eight day old Jewish boy marking his entry into the covenantal community.

Bubbe—*(Yiddish)* Grandmother.

Chazzan—Cantor.

Drek—*(Yiddish)* Filth, excrement.

---

* All glossed words are Hebrew, unless otherwise noted.

Egged—Israeli state bus company.

Ehrliche chazzunim—*(Yiddish)* Fine, upstanding cantors.

Einsatzgruppen—*(German)* Squads that carried out mass killings of Jews, such as at Babi Yar.

Eleh Ezkerah—"These I Shall Remember," a prayer of the Yom Kippur liturgy that describes the martyrdom of ten great rabbinic Sages who died at the hands of Roman Emperor Vespasian. He claimed he was merely punishing the Sages for the crime of their ancestors, the eleven brothers who sold Joseph into slavery. One rabbinic commentary suggests that the brothers traded Joseph for a pair of sandals.

Elijah's chair—The prophet Elijah, bearer of good tidings and herald of the Messiah, is believed to attend every bris. Thus, a special chair is set aside for him.

Eruv—One type of work forbidden on the Sabbath is the transporting or carrying of objects in the public domain. However, an ad hoc construction (the *eruv*) that creates a perimeter around a physical space symbolically transforms that space into a "private" domain; one is then permitted to carry objects within that "private" area. This is a feature of many Jewish neighborhoods.

Gadol hador—a giant of the generation in religious scholarship.

Hagomel lechayavim tovot—A special blessing of thanksgiving recited by one who recently emerged safely from an illness, accident or dangerous journey.

Halachah—Jewish law, the Jewish way.

Hondle—(*Yiddish*) Make deals.

Illui—Young genius, well versed in Talmud.

116

Glossary

Kapo—*(German)* Concentration camp prisoner-guard, often unsavory type.

Kest—*(Yiddish)* Marriage dowry, given to scholars to support their families while they continued to study Torah.

Ketubah—The Jewish marriage contract.

Kippot—Skullcaps, yarmulkes.

Le Chambon—A town in southeast France whose five thousand French Huguenot inhabitants sheltered and saved five thousand Jews fleeing the Nazis.

Lehadlik ner—Blessing recited upon lighting the Sabbath and Holiday candles.

Levir—Biblical law required a man (the levir) to marry the widow of his deceased brother in the event that the brother had died childless. The rabbis subsequently proscribed levirate marriages.

Leysheyv basukkah—The blessing recited upon sitting in the sukkah, the temporary booth erected each year for the fall holiday of Sukkot which commemorates the Israelites' wandering in the wilderness for 40 years.

Maariv—The evening prayer service.

Macht a bruchah—*(Yiddish)* Recite a blessing.

Mah nishtanah—"Why is it [this night] different?" Opening phrase of the famous Four Questions, asked by the child at the Passover seder.

Malbish arumim—"Who clothes the naked." Blessing recited each morning and also on the occasion of donning a new garment for the first time.

Mazel tov—Congratulations! Good fortune!

Mikvah—The ritual pool or bath in which Jewish women immerse themselves following a period of sexual separation that began with onset of menses. After the menses and an additional five day waiting period, immersion is required before a couple may resume marital relations.

Minchah—The afternoon prayer service.

Mohel—One who performs the circumcision.

Musaf—The additional prayer service recited on the Sabbath and other holy days.

Nagymama—(*Hungarian*) Grandmother.

Neilah—An intense prayer service, recited at the closing of Yom Kippur. Repentance is its theme.

Pesach—Passover. The celebration of the Exodus from Egypt.

Rabban, Rav, **Rebbe**—Rabbi; Teacher.

Rebbetzin—(*Yiddish*) Rabbi's wife.

Sandek—A guest at a circumcision ceremony who is given the honor of holding the baby while the mohel performs the rite.

Shmooze—(*Yiddish*) Chat.

Sefer Torah—Torah scroll.

Shabbat, Shabbos—The Sabbath.

Shacharis—The morning prayer service.

Shalleshudos—Third Sabbath meal.

Shavuot—Pentecost. The festival celebrating Revelation and the giving of the Torah at Sinai.

Glossary

Shaylos—Questions, usually of a religious nature, brought to a rabbi for a decision.

Shehakol nihyeh bidvaro—Blessing recited prior to eating or drinking certain foods and beverages.

Sheitel—*(Yiddish)* Wig, worn by married Jewish women as a sign of modesty.

Shelo chisar beolamo—Blessing recited upon seeing the first blossoms of spring.

Shema—The central Jewish prayer affirming belief in one God.

Shenatan mechachmato—Blessing recited upon encountering great scholars of secular learning.

Shiva—The seven-day mourning period following the death of an immediate relative. The mourners sit at home on low stools and receive visits of consolation from friends and relatives.

Shtetl—Small town, village.

Shtill—Quiet, silence.

Shul—Synagogue

Simchat Bat—Celebration upon the occassion of the birth of a baby girl, welcoming her into the covenantal community.

Tante—(*Yiddish*) Aunt.

Tefillah—Prayer.

Tefillin—Phylacteries (prayer boxes containing sacred texts). Tefillin are worn during morning prayers, strapped to the head and arm with leather bindings. When not in use, they are frequently stored in a velvet bag.

Tevilah—Immersion in the mikvah.

Tref—Non-kosher, non permissible foods.

Tisha B'Av—The ninth day of the Hebrew month of Av, a fast day commemorating the destruction of the Holy Temple of Jerusalem, in 586 B.C.E. and again in 70 C.E..

Trocmé—Protestant minister of Le Chambon and his wife (André and Magda) who led the townspeople in hiding Jews during World War II.

Yasom—Orphan.

Yeshiva—Traditional academy of rabbinical studies.

Yeshiva bochur—(*Yiddish*) Student at a Yeshiva

Yevamot—Levirs. *See* Levir

Yidden—(*Yiddish*) Jews.

Yiddishkeit—(*Yiddish*) Judaism, Jewishness.

Yom Hashoah—Annual day of commemoration of the Holocaust (*shoah*).

Yom Kippur—Day of Atonement.

Zayde—(*Yiddish*) Grandfather.

Zielna—One of the main streets in the Jewish area of Warsaw before the War.

Zocher habrit—"Who remembers the covenant"; the blessing recited upon seeing a rainbow. It summons up the rainbow that appeared after the Flood, a symbol of the covenant with Noah in which God promised never again to destroy the world by flood.